A Bilingual Book
English/Español

¡can read **Bible Stories**

Joash
the Boy King

Rose Tooley Gamblin
and
Oscar Hernandéz

Autumn House® Publishing
www.autumnhousepublishing.com
A Division of **REVIEW AND HERALD® PUBLISHING**
Since 1861

Published by Autumn House® Publishing, a division of Review and Herald®
Publishing, Hagerstown, MD 21741-1119

Autumn House® titles may be purchased in bulk for educational, business,
fund-raising, or sales promotional use. For information, please e-mail
SpecialMarkets@reviewandherald.com.

Autumn House® Publishing publishes biblically based materials for spiritual,
physical, and mental growth and Christian discipleship.

The author assumes full responsibility for the accuracy of all facts and
quotations as cited in this book.

This book was
       Edited by Jeannette R. Johnson
       Designed by Ron Pride and Tricia Wegh
       Art by Robert Berran
       Typeset: Clearface Regular 16/24

PRINTED IN U.S.A.

12 11 10 09 08   5 4 3 2 1

Library of Congress Cataloging-in-Publication Data

Gamblin, Rose Tooley, 1956-   .
  Joash, the boy king / Rose Tooley Gamblin and Oscar Hernandéz.
     p. cm. – (I can read Bible stories books)
  English and Spanish.
  1. Joash, King of Judah—Juvenile literature. 2. Bible Stories, English—O.T.
Kings, 2nd. 3. Bible. O.T. Kings, 2nd XI-XII, 16 Biography—Juvenile literature.
I. Hernandéz, Oscar. II. Title.

BS580.J48G36 2007
222'.54092—dc22

2007043060

ISBN 978-0-8127-0474-7

This book is dedicated to
Brennan Marté

I have read this book all by myself!
¡He leído este libro todo por mi mismo.

_____

My Name / Mi Nombre

_____

Date / Fecha

What I Think About This Story
Qué Pienso De Esta Historia

_____

_____

_____

_____

Other *Bible Stories* Books:

Baby Moses
Esther the Brave Queen
King David
The Queen of Sheba
King Jesus

To order, call
1-800-765-6955.

Visit us at
www.AutumnHousePublishing.com
for information on other Autumn House® products.

Dear Caring Adult:

Thank you for choosing an *I-Can-Read* bilingual book for your child!

It is the desire of the authors that this book will:

1. Provide meaningful reading material for a beginner reader. Now they can read to their parents or younger siblings!
2. Encourage a love for reading by giving the child ownership of their own *I-Can-Read* book.
3. Provide an important multicultural lesson by exposing them to another language.
4. Become a child's best friend, leading them to Jesus.

What better way to soften the nighttime jitters than to send your child to bed with thoughts of God's love.

—The Publishers

Apreciado padre o maestro:

Lo felicitamos por poner en manos de sus pequeñitos el libro bilingüe *Yo puedo leer*, y deseamos que sea éste el primer libro que ellos puedan leer.

Nuestro objetivo es llenar una necesidad palpable dentro de la población latina radicada en Norteamérica. Nuestros niños, desde que nacen están expuestos tanto al español como al inglés; por lo tanto, buscamos que ellos aprendan a leer en ambos idiomas y que amen así la lectura. Pero más que leer, nuestro objetivo ulterior es que desde sus primeros años sean expuestos a Jesús, el Salvador de la humanidad, y que crezcan amando al mejor Amigo de los niños.

—Los editores

The baby is crying.
"Don't cry, Baby Joash!
Don't let the bad queen hear you."

El bebé está llorando
"¡No llores, bebé Joás!
No dejes que te escuche la reina mala."

Look at the boy.

He is not a baby.

He is a big boy!

He is Joash!

Mira al chico.
Él no es un bebé.
Él es un muchacho grande.
Él es Joás.

See the wall of God's house?
The wall needs to be fixed.
Who will fix it?

¿Ves la pared de la casa de Dios?
La pared necesita reparación.
¿Quién la reparará?

Joash can read.

Uncle can read.

They read about God.

Joás puede leer.
El tío puede leer.
Ellos leen de Dios.

Here is Joash.

Here is Uncle.

What will happen?

Aquí está Joás.
Aquí está el tío.
¿Qué sucederá?

Here is Joash.

Here is Uncle.

Joash will be king!

Aquí está Joás.
Aquí está el tío.
¡Joás será el rey!

"¡Ay, no!" dijo el tío.
"¡Ay, no!" dijo el rey Joás.
¡Viene la reina mala!

"Oh, no!" said Uncle.

"Oh, no!" said King Joash.

The bad queen is coming!

See King Joash.
The men can help.
The bad queen is gone.

Mira al rey Joás.
Los hombres pueden ayudar.
La reina mala se fue.

"I will fix the wall,"
said King Joash.
"I will fix the wall of God's house."

"Yo repararé la pared,"
dijo el rey Joás.
"Yo repararé la pared de la casa de Dios."

"I can help!" said the boy.
"I can help!" said the girl.
"We can all help fix the wall
of God's house!"

"Yo puedo ayudar," dijo el chico.
"Yo puedo ayudar," dijo la chica.
"Nosotros todos podemos ayudar
a reparar la pared de la casa de Dios."

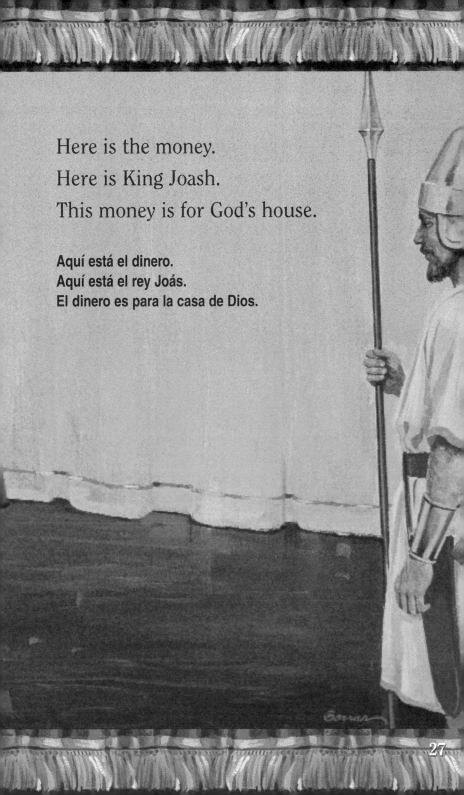

Here is the money.
Here is King Joash.
This money is for God's house.

Aquí está el dinero.
Aquí está el rey Joás.
El dinero es para la casa de Dios.

God's house is fixed.

God is happy.

King Joash is happy.

La casa de Dios ha sido reparada.
Dios está feliz.
El rey Joás está feliz.

Words in This Book

a (un/una)

about (de)

all (todo)

at (en)

baby (bebé)

bad (mala)

be (ser/estar)

big (grande)

boy (chico)

can (poder)

coming (viniendo)

cry (llorar)

crying (llorando)

don't (no)

fix (reparar)

fixed (reparada)

for (para)

girl (niña)

God (Dios)

God's (de Dios)

gone (fue)

happen (suceder)

happy (feliz)

he (él)

hear (escushar)

help (ayudar)

here (aquí)

house (casa)

I (yo)

is (está)

it

Joash (Joás)

king (rey)

let (dejar-permitir)

look (mirar)

men (hombres)

money (dinero)

needs (necesita)

no (no)

not (no)

of (de)

oh (ay)

queen (reina)

read (leer)

said (dijo)

see (ver)

the (la/el)

they (ellos)

this (esto)

to (a)

Uncle (tío)

wall (pared)

we (nosotros)

what (que)

who (quién)

will

you (tú)

Note: There are 57 words in this book. RL:1.0. The Spanish vocabulary reflects the meaning as used in this book.

El vocabulario español refleja el significdado según lo utilizado en este libro.

What Do You Think?

1. Why did the walls need to be fixed?
2. Whom was Joash reading about?
3. Why did the men need spears?
4. What would you have done if you were made king?
5. How can you fix God's house?

Additional Activities

1. Using Legos, or other blocks, make a temple.
2. Find the country of Israel in a Bible atlas.
3. Make a bank out of an empty container and see how much money you can save in one week. Give the money to your church.
4. Find the story of Joash, the boy king, in the Bible.
5. Choose words from the word list and make up your own picture story.
6. Write a poem and say it for family worship.